First published in Great Britain in 1992 by
Michael O'Mara Books Limited,
9 Lion Yard, Tremadoc Road, London SW4 7NQ
in association with
Independent Television News Limited

A CIP catalogue record for this book is available from the British Library

ISBN 1-85479-146-X

Designed and typeset by Martin Bristow

Edited by Fiona Holman

Printed and bound in Hong Kong
by Paramount Printing Group Limited

ITN

THE ROYAL YEAR 1992

PHOTOGRAPHED BY TIM GRAHAM

MICHAEL O'MARA BOOKS LIMITED
in association with
INDEPENDENT TELEVISION NEWS LIMITED

On a rainy day in early July the Princess of Wales paid a visit to Blackpool in Lancashire, where she visited the Lyons Biscuit Factory and donned protective clothing to tour the factory floor. She also visited youth projects and a workshop for the blind.

Right and below left: Torrential rain in Blackpool on 2 July did not prevent the Princess of Wales from laughing and joking with the waiting crowds as she travelled between engagements. Below right: Arriving at the Banqueting House in central London on 3 July for a gala concert in aid of Help the Hospices Association.

On 3 July the Duke of York paid a visit to the Duke of York's Royal Military School at Dover for the School's Grand Day. During Trooping of the Colour the Duke took the Salute. He also had an opportunity of talking to some Chelsea Pensioners.

Facing page: A day out for Princess Beatrice at the Royal Berkshire Polo Club where the Duchess of York was presenting the prizes.
Above left: Princess Margaret visited the world-famous Kew Gardens on 10 July to open a new Marine Display.
Above right: The Princess of Wales leaving the Royal Tournament after taking Princes William and Harry for a summer holiday treat.
Right: The Princess of Wales took Mrs Barbara Bush to the Middlesex Hospital in central London on 17 July to meet patients suffering from Aids.

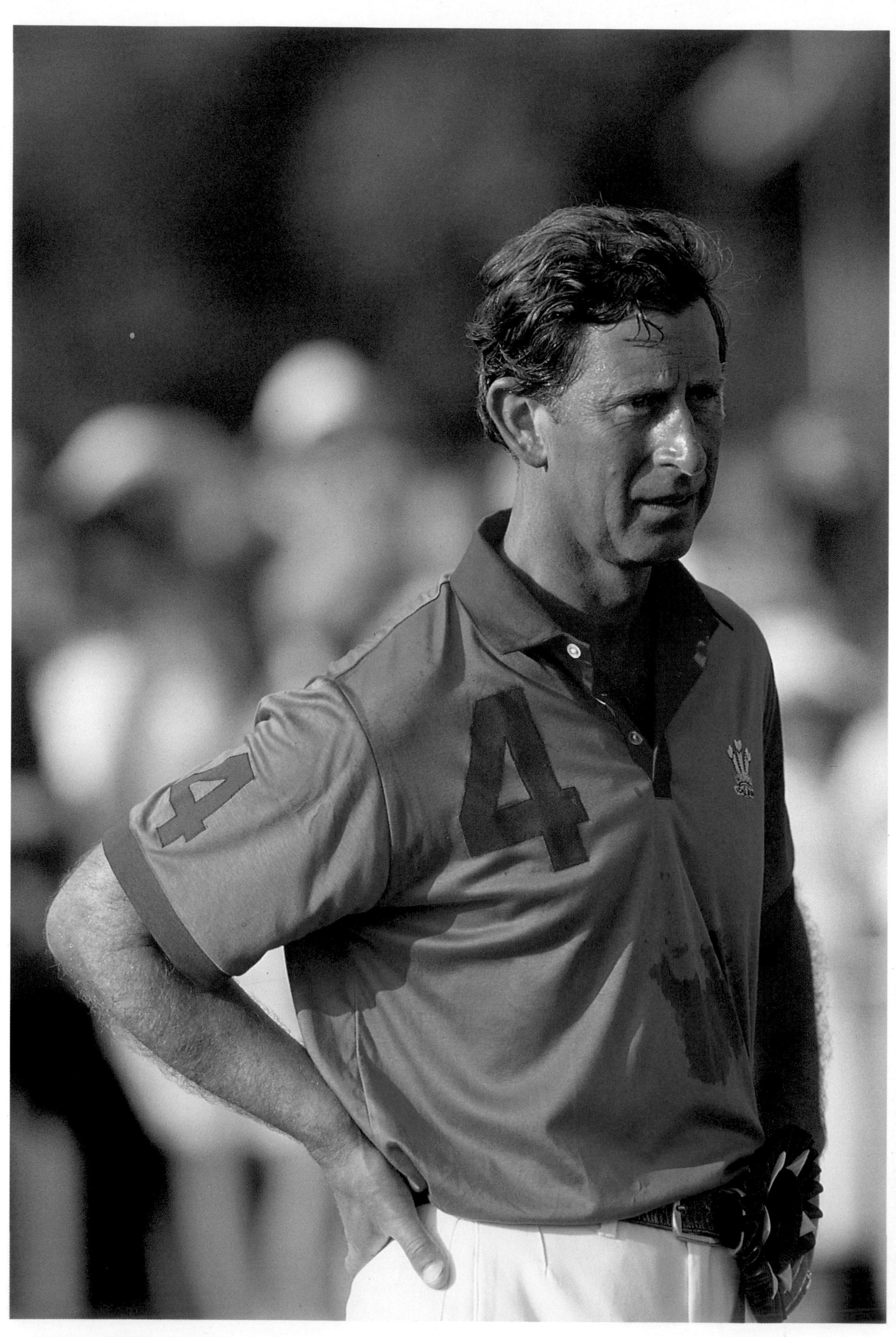
4
4

Facing page: Prince Charles at the Cartier International Polo on 28 July, the highlight of the English polo season.
Right and below left: The Queen entertained President and Mrs Gorbachev at Buckingham Palace on 18 July.
Below right: The Duchess of York at the marina, Chelsea Harbour for a charity car rally on behalf of the Chemical Dependency Centre.

A drenched Princess of Wales and more than 100,000 fans defied a downpour to listen to the world's greatest tenor, Luciano Pavarotti sing at an open air concert in Hyde Park to celebrate his 30th anniversary in opera. After the concert the royal party went backstage and the Princess of Wales jokingly remarked to Pavarotti that he was drier than they were.

On 4 August the Queen Mother celebrated her 91st birthday quietly at Sandringham in Norfolk by going to morning service at the local parish church. After the service the Queen and Queen Mother were greeted by local children waiting outside the lych gate.

Facing page: A family group at Kensington Palace to commemorate the 90th year of Princess Alice, Duchess of Gloucester. With Princess Alice are her son and daughter-in-law, the Duke and Duchess of Gloucester, and their children, the Lady Rose Windsor (left), the Lady Davina Windsor (right) and the Earl of Ulster.
Right: The Queen and Prince Edward waving from HMY Britannia *as the ship sets sail from Portsmouth for the Queen's annual cruise to the Western Isles of Scotland.*
Below left: Peter Phillips driving a Honda tractor at his Gloucestershire home during the Gatcombe Horse Trials.
Below right: The Princess of Wales and Prince William leaving Wetherby School after taking Prince Harry back to school on 5 September.

Above left: On 6 September the Princess of Wales visited Salisbury with the Prince of Wales for a charity concert to help restore one of Britain's most magnificent cathedrals.
Above right: Princess Beatrice wearing a smart blue uniform on her first day at Windsor's Upton House School accompanied by the Duchess of York.
Right: On 16 September the Prince of Wales and the Crown Prince Naruhito of Japan, joint patrons of the Japan Festival 1991, a five-month long celebration of Japanese culture up and down the country, opened an exhibition of Japanese Robot Technology in South Kensington.

Left: The Duke of York, Colonel-in-Chief of the Staffordshire Regiment, attended a Gulf Thanksgiving Service at Lichfield Cathedral on 20 September. Right and below: The Princess of Wales at the charity première of Stepping Out *at the Empire Cinema, Leicester Square.*

THE PRINCESS OF WALES VISITS PAKISTAN

23 – 27 September 1991

The Princess of Wales's highly successful trip to Pakistan was her longest solo official visit abroad. During the hectic five-day visit the Princess enjoyed the sights and sounds of this colourful country, including a visit to the spectacular Khyber Pass.

Right: For her arrival in Islamabad, the modern capital of Pakistan, the Princess of Wales wore pale green and white, a diplomatic reference to the country's national colours.
Facing page and below: On the second day of the tour the Princess, wearing a traditional garland of tinsel, visited a family welfare centre at Noopur Shahan. On her arrival children scattered flower petals in her path, another colourful Pakistani custom.

Facing page far left: Wearing a beaded pale pink dress for dinner with the President of Pakistan.
Facing page left: Touring the great Mogul mosque of Badshahi in Lahore, and in accordance with Muslim custom the Princess removed her shoes.
Facing page below: The Princess being greeted by the students of the Kinnaird College for Women.

Left: At the Kinnaird College for Women.
Below left. At the Shishmahal, Lahore Fort, wearing another colourful garland.
Below right: For the visit to the Badshahi mosque in Lahore the Princess covered her head with a gold-embroidered shawl to respect Muslim tradition.

Facing page: The Princess of Wales posing with men of the Khyber Rifles at Michni Point in the Khyber Pass which is on the border with Afghanistan.
Above: The Duchess of York, as patron of the Sick Children's Trust, unveiling a plaque at the opening of the Trust's fourth 'Home from Home'.
Above right: The Princess of Wales in Banbury, Oxfordshire on 14 October.
Right: The Duchess of Kent talking to staff and patients at the opening of Bishop's Wood Private Hospital in Northwood, Middlesex.

THE WALES FAMILY ON TOUR IN CANADA

23 – 29 October 1991

For the first time Princes William and Harry accompanied the Prince and Princess of Wales abroad on a royal tour. While the Prince and Princess of Wales carried out their own official engagements the royal princes were taken on sightseeing expeditions in and around Toronto. HMY Britannia, moored on Lake Ontario, served as 'home from home' for the boys who were on their half-term holiday.

Above: The Princess of Wales arriving in Toronto, wearing a striking red, black and white suit. Left: Princes William and Harry arriving on board Britannia *one day ahead of their parents. Facing page: Disembarking from HMCS* Ottawa *after a riveting tour of the Canadian frigate, which was moored near* Britannia *on Lake Ontario. During the visit the princes were presented with badges and gold-braided baseball caps embroidered with the ship's name.*

HMCS OTTAWA
DDH 229
HMCS OTTAWA
DDH 229

Left: Wearing a white safety helmet and goggles, the Prince of Wales toured the INCO smelting works near Sudbury, a polluted mining town in northern Ontario, and inaugurated a new environmental control project in the smelter.
Below: At the official welcome to Ontario at Science Youth Centre, Sudbury.
Right: A wet walkabout at Sudbury airport for the Princess of Wales.

Above: The Prince and Princess of Wales at Toronto City Hall for the civic welcoming ceremony.
Left: The Princess of Wales leaving the Royal Alexandra Theatre after a performance of the hit musical, Les Misérables.
Right: At the gala evening organized by United World Colleges and ABC Canada at the Royal York Hotel.
Facing page: Earlier in the day the Princess of Wales took the two excited princes to see the spectacular Niagara Falls on the Canadian-US border just two hours' drive from Toronto. Wearing bright blue oilskins to protect them from the heavy spray the royal party inspected the Falls on board the tour boat, Maid of the Mist.

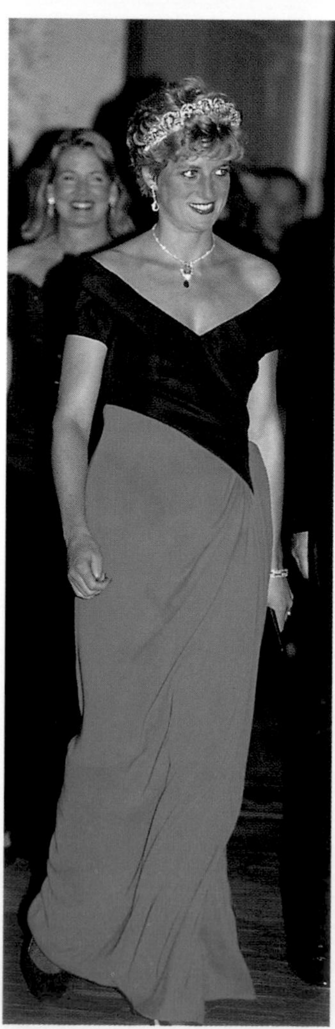

MAID OF THE MIST

MAID OF THE MIST

Above: Princes William (right) and Harry (left) greet the crowds after attending Sunday morning service at St James Anglican Cathedral in Toronto.
Left: Waving farewell to Toronto as Britannia *sets sail for Kingston, its next port of call. That evening the princes flew back home while the Prince and Princess of Wales remained in Canada for a further two days of engagements.*
Facing page above left: The Princess of Wales at the Rideaucrest Home in Kingston. Above right: The Prince of Wales was presented with an honorary doctorate at Queen's University. Facing page below: Inspecting the Princess of Wales' Own Regiment at Kingston Armoury.

Above: The Prince and Princess of Wales at Rideau Hall in Ottawa for an official lunch hosted by the Governor-General of Canada.
Right and facing page: The Princess of Wales at the National Arts Centre for a concert given in the royal couple's honour by the Prime Minister of Canada and Mrs Mulroney.

Left: The Princess of Wales garlanded with flowers at the opening of the Sangam Association of Asian Women's community centre in Edgware, Middlesex on 18 November. Facing page above: The Duchess of York at the departure of Dreamflight from Heathrow Airport when 200 seriously ill children left for the holiday of a lifetime at Disney World in Florida. Right: The Princess of Wales, as patron, Help the Aged, arriving for a gala performance of Verdi's Simon Boccanegra *at the Royal Opera House, Covent Garden. Far right: On 14 November the Queen Mother visited the new Friends of the Tate Room at the Tate Gallery.*

ISH AIRWAYS

Tigger
WELSH

Right: The Princess of Wales at the Royal Film Performance of Hot Shots at the Odeon Cinema, Leicester Square.
Below: The Queen receiving the President of Hungary at Buckingham Palace.

Facing page right: Prince Edward visiting Booth Hall Children's Hospital in Manchester, one of the largest children's hospitals in the country.
Facing page below left: Princess Alexandra meeting a hedgehog at the St Tiggywinkle's Wildlife Hospital in Aylesbury, Buckinghamshire.
Facing page below right: The Princess of Wales in a stunning, multi-coloured suit for a charity rock concert given by the Chicken Shed Theatre Company at the Empire Ballroom, Leicester Square on 28 November.

THE PRINCESS ROYAL VISITS THE MIDDLE EAST

2 – 5 December 1991

In early December the Princess Royal made a whistlestop tour of the Gulf, visiting the United Arab Emirates, Qatar, Bahrain and Kuwait in the space of four days, with engagements each morning, afternoon and evening.

Above: The Princess Royal in Qatar.
Left: Reviewing a parade in Abu Dhabi to commemorate the 20th anniversary of the United Arab Emirates.

Facing page above: Visiting the schoolroom in the Rumaillah hospital in Qatar.
Facing page below: British children giving the Princess Royal a rousing welcome outside the British Council offices in Qatar.

السبت
الأحد
الإثنين
الثلاثاء
الأربعاء
الخميس
الجمعة
أنا
في
المدرسة
أهلاً أهلاً أهلاً
التعليم الخاص
الرميلة
قسم التعليم
الخاص
SP·Ed

Above: The Princess Royal with the Crown Prince of Bahrain, Sheikh Hamad Bin Isa Salman Al Kalifa at the Al Areen Wildlife Park in Bahrain.
Left: Meeting pupils at St Christopher's School in Isa Town, Bahrain.

Above left: The Princess Royal's one-day visit to Kuwait included a tour of the Kuwait English School.
Above right: Inspecting bombs and mines left over from the occupation of Kuwait by the Iraqi forces, at the Royal Ordnance Camp at Masseela.
Right: Talking to children and parents at the Kuwait English School.

Right and below left: The Princess of Wales took Princes William and Harry along with her to the 'Joy to the World' Christmas carol concert at the Royal Albert Hall in aid of the Royal Marsden Hospital's appeal for cancer research.

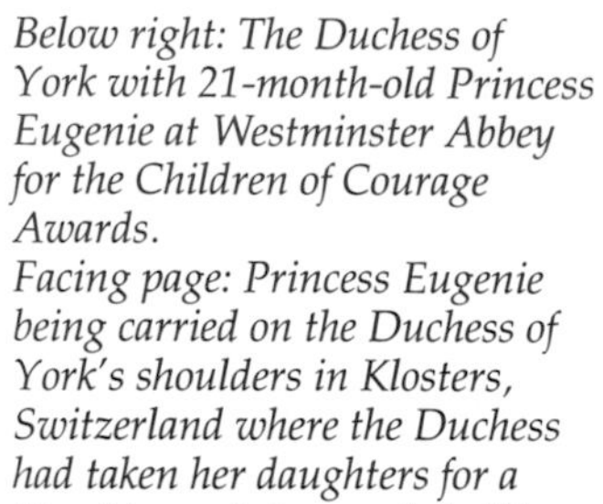

Below right: The Duchess of York with 21-month-old Princess Eugenie at Westminster Abbey for the Children of Courage Awards.
Facing page: Princess Eugenie being carried on the Duchess of York's shoulders in Klosters, Switzerland where the Duchess had taken her daughters for a New Year winter sports holiday.

Facing page: Princess Beatrice, who was still recovering from a pre-Christmas attack of chicken pox, with ski guide and friend Bruno Sprecher, and taking tentative steps on skis, helped by the Duchess of York. Princess Eugenie, too young to learn to ski, enjoyed a spot of tobogganing with her sister and mother.
Above: Lady Helen Windsor, daughter of the Duke and Duchess of Kent, announced her engagement to Mr Tim Taylor on 7 January.
Left: The Princess of Wales and Prince William leaving Wetherby School, having delivered Prince Harry back to school after the Christmas holidays.
Right: The Princess of Wales, as patron, arriving at the Lanesborough Hotel, central London, for a charity lunch in aid of British Red Cross Youth.

Above left: The Duchess of York at the launch of 'Tommy's Campaign' in aid of the Baby Fund at St Thomas's Hospital, central London.
Above right: The Princess of Wales, as patron, visiting the London Deaf Video Project organized by the British Deaf Association.

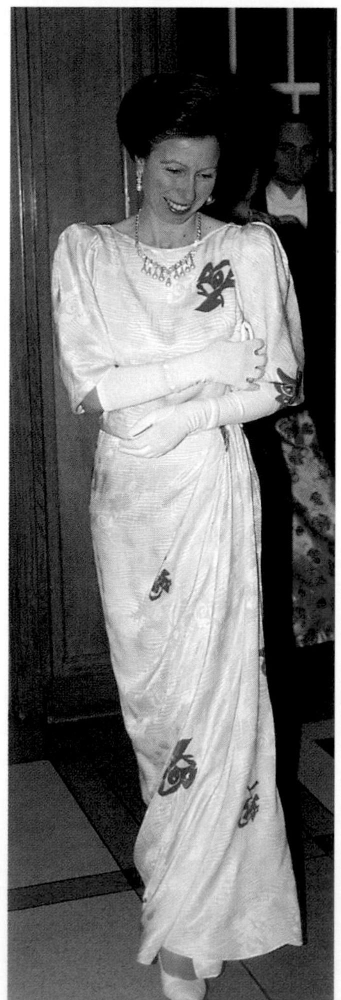

Far left: The Princess Royal arriving for a livery dinner at Painters' Hall in the City of London on 15 January.
Left: The following evening the Princess of Wales, patron of the London Symphony Chorus, attended a Beethoven concert at the Barbican Centre.
Facing page: The Princess of Wales was back at the Barbican on 23 January for the Hong Kong Gala Evening.

Facing page left: Princess Michael of Kent went to Piccadilly on 31 January to unveil London's newest landmark sculpture, 'The Horses of Helios'.
Facing page right: The Princess of Wales at Stratford-upon-Avon in Warwickshire on 4 February.
Facing page below: On the 40th anniversary of her accession to the Throne, 6 February 1992, the Queen paid a quiet visit to Tapping House at Snettisham, Norfolk, the day centre for the West Norfolk Home Hospice Support Group.

Right and below: The Duchess of Gloucester opened the new Children's Block of St Bartholomew's Hospital in London on 28 January and afterwards visited children on the wards.

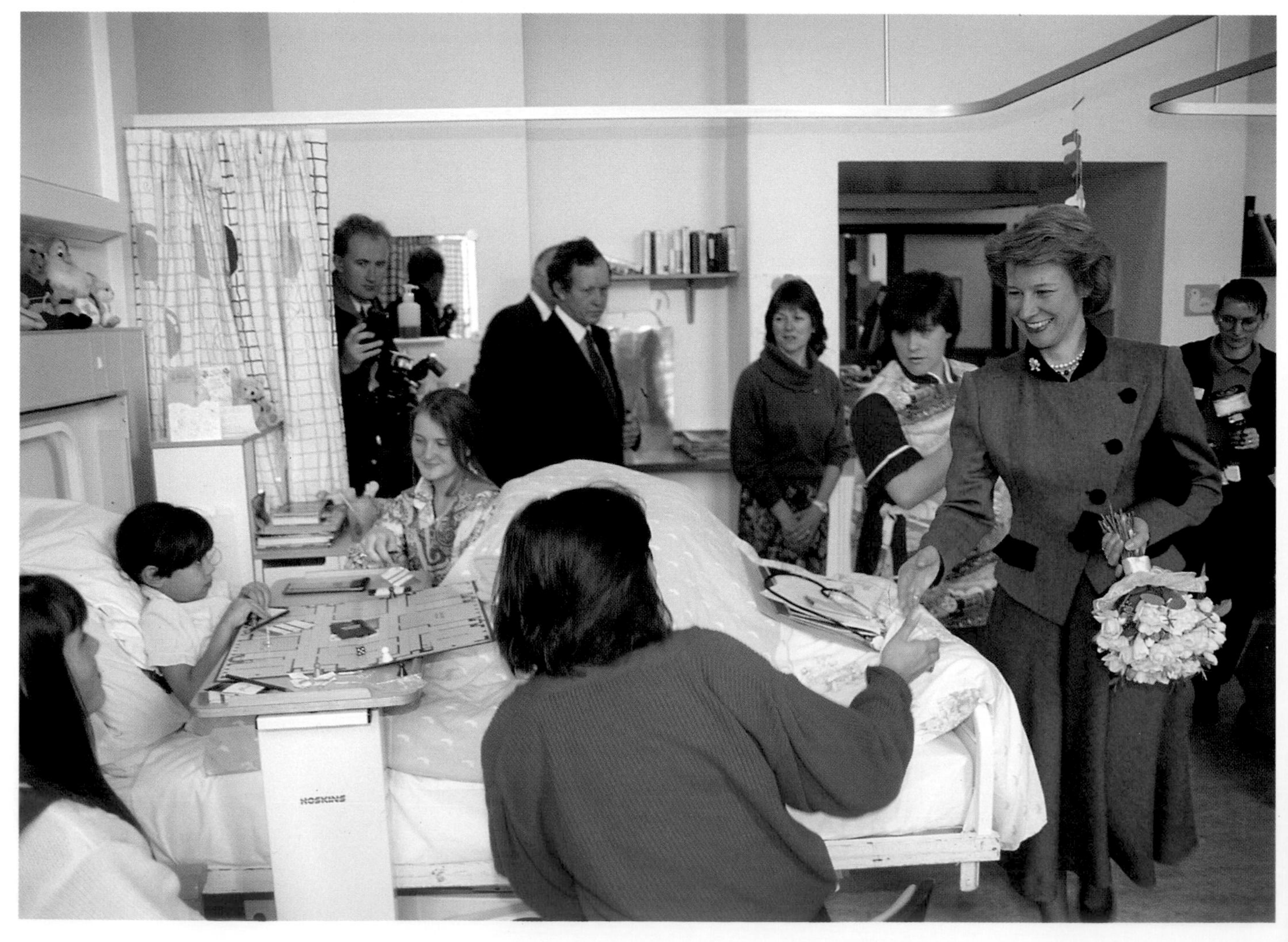

THE PRINCE AND PRINCESS OF WALES VISIT INDIA

10 – 15 February 1992

The couple's first visit together to India, postponed for a year because of the Gulf War, began with a series of official engagements in the capital, Delhi, but there were opportunities during the hectic week for the royal couple to see the real India, away from the ceremony and red carpets that go with all royal tours.

Facing page above: The Princess of Wales at Parivar Seva Sanstha, the Indian branch of the Marie Stopes family planning organization.
Facing page below: The Prince of Wales inspecting the Guard of Honour at Rashtrapati Bhavan, the official residence of the President of India.
Overleaf: Posing for photographers at the Taj Mahal, the 17th-century mausoleum built by Shah Jehan for his favourite wife.

Right: Laying a wreath at Raj Ghat, the memorial to Mahatma Gandhi.
Below left and right: The Princess of Wales visiting the Tamana Special Nursery School for handicapped children, whose new building the Princess had helped pay for.

Right and below: On 13 February the Prince and Princess of Wales paid a joint visit to the rural village of Nalu west of Jaipur to inspect local development projects. On their arrival colourfully dressed peasant women lightly brushed the Princess's feet and ankles with their fingers as a mark of respect.

Facing page: While in Jaipur the Prince of Wales spent an afternoon playing polo and was delighted to score three out of four goals for the winning side. The Princess of Wales arrived at the polo ground in time to see Prince Charles's victory and to present him with the silver Poonglia Cup.
Overleaf: Watching a display of dancing at Lallapet High School in Hyderabad.

3
4

Facing page above: Meeting the Untouchables, India's lowest caste, at the Mianpur Old Age Welfare Centre in Hyderabad. Facing page below and this page: One of the most memorable engagements of the Princess's stay in India was the visit to Mother Teresa's Missionaries of Charity in Calcutta. She toured Mother Teresa's Home for Abandoned Children and the Hospice for the Dying. Mother Teresa has cared for Calcutta's poor and dying for the past 40 years but sadly for the Princess who was longing to meet her, Mother Teresa was still recovering from a mild heart attack in Rome.

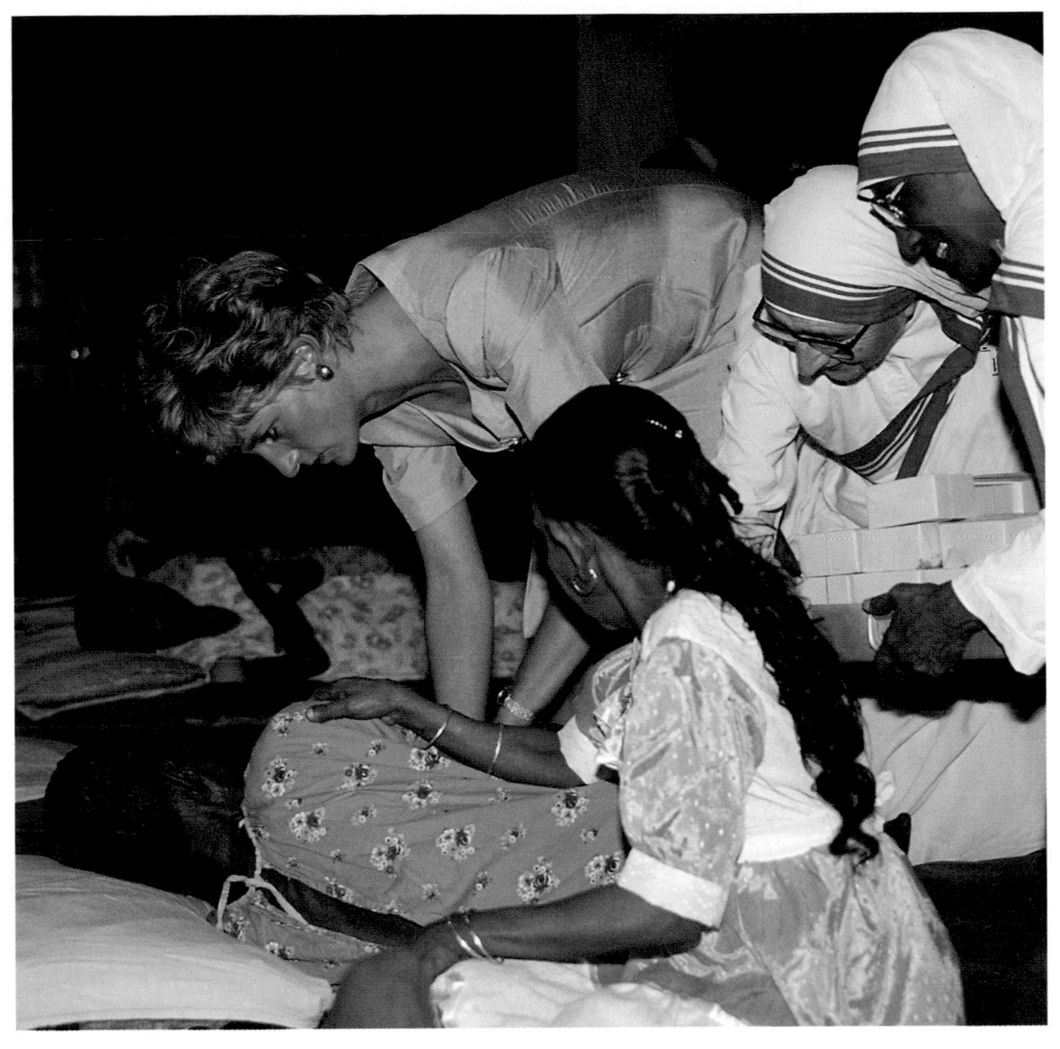

Facing page above: The Princess of Wales meeting the film stars, Nick Nolte and Barbra Streisand at the charity première of their new film, Prince of Tides *on 18 February.*
Facing page below: Prince and Princess Michael of Kent at the Grosvenor House Hotel, central London for the glittering fashion gala, 'Shocking Pink', held on 24 February to mark Oxfam's 50th anniversary.

Right above: On 4 March the Princess of Wales presented the Children of Europe Awards at the Savoy Hotel, central London. Twelve children, one from each of the EC countries, received awards for bravery, including Irene Villa, a Spanish bomb victim.
Right: The Princess of Wales, President of Barnados, greeting crowds outside the Dudley Family Centre in the West Midlands, one of the charity's 155 projects nationwide.

Left: The Queen went to Reading University in Berkshire on 6 March to celebrate the 100th anniversary of higher education in the town.
Below left: The Queen at this year's Commonwealth Day Observance Service held in Westminster Abbey on 9 March.
Below right: On 17 March the Princess visited the city of Lincoln, accompanied by the Prince of Wales.

Right: On 23 March the Princess of Wales paid a two-day visit to Budapest, Hungary, during which she went to the world-famous Peto Institute which has pioneered conductive education for the treatment of cerebral palsy. Below: Meeting Croatian refugees who have crossed the border into Hungary to escape the bitter fighting in Yugoslavia.

Left: At the State Opera House in Budapest for a gala performance by English National Ballet, of which the Princess is Patron. Facing page: The Princess of Wales sympathising with Croatian refugees at the Nagyatad Refugee Camp on the Yugoslav border with Hungary.

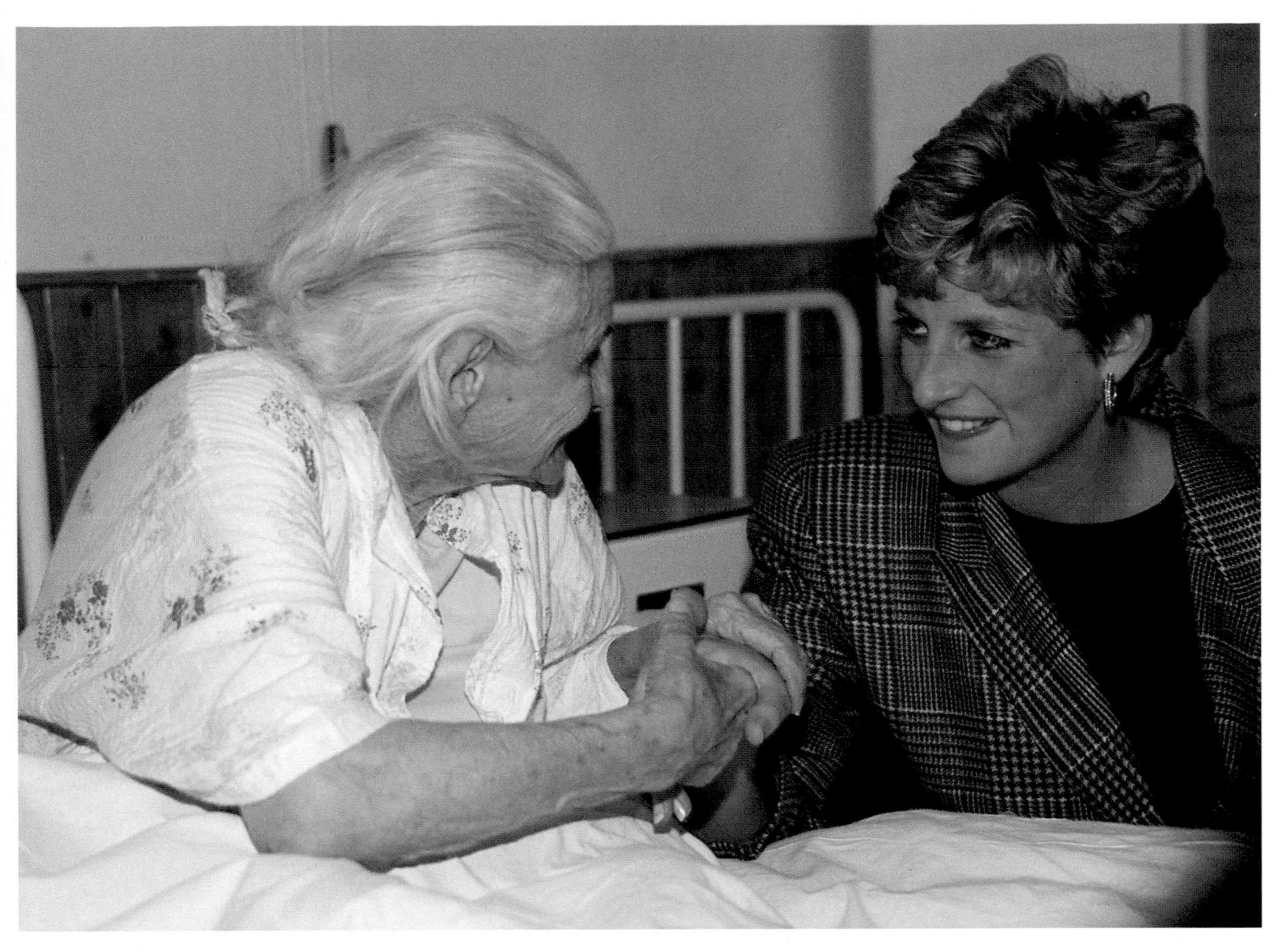

At the end of March the Princess of Wales took Prince William and Prince Harry on their second skiing holiday to Lech in Austria. The princes spent a few days practising on the slopes before the Prince of Wales arrived to join the family for the second part of the holiday.

Facing page: On 10 April Princess Alexandra represented the Queen at the Sovereign's Parade at the Royal Military Academy, Sandhurst.
Right: Prince Harry leaving the Natural History Museum on 13 April when he accompanied the Princess of Wales, patron of the Museum, and Prince William for an Easter holiday treat to the official opening of the new Dinosaur Gallery.

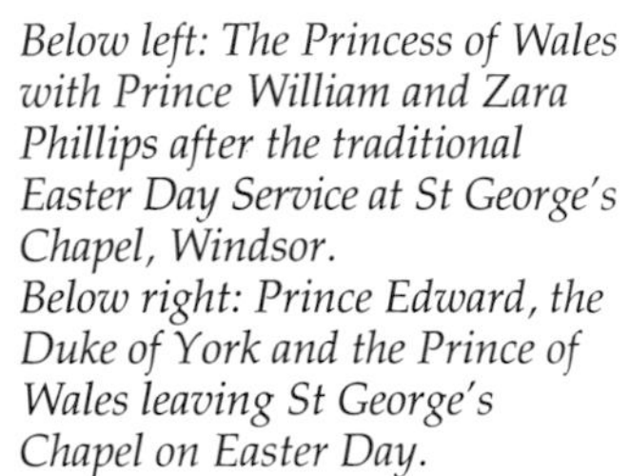

Below left: The Princess of Wales with Prince William and Zara Phillips after the traditional Easter Day Service at St George's Chapel, Windsor.
Below right: Prince Edward, the Duke of York and the Prince of Wales leaving St George's Chapel on Easter Day.

Right: The Princess Royal, a keen sailor for many years, visited the Solent on 24 April as patron of the British Steel Challenge Round the World Yacht Race 1992 to take part in a day's sailing with the fleet of yachts competing in the race.

Below: A delighted patient meets the Princess of Wales at the Babington Hospital Day Unit, Belper during the Princess's visit to Derbyshire on 28 April.

Right: The Princess of Wales laughing during her visit to Derbyshire.

Below left: Princess Margaret at the Curzon Cinema, Mayfair for the gala film première of Howard's End *on 28 April.*
Below right: The Prince of Wales waving to onlookers during his visit to the 1992 National Garden Festival which he officially opened on 5 May at Ebbw Vale, Gwent, Wales.

Left: On 6 May the Princess of Wales attended an evening gala at Spencer House in St James's, central London as patron of the London City Ballet. Spencer House overlooking Green Park is the former London home of the Spencer family and has recently undergone a magnificent restoration.
Below: The Queen accompanied by Prince Philip went to Westminster on 6 May for the State Opening of the new Parliament following the general election in April.

On 8 May the Princess Royal, wearing striking blue jockey's silks, rode Bengal Tiger in the 3.30 race at Lingfield Park, Surrey.

THE PRINCESS OF WALES VISITS EGYPT

10 – 15 May 1992

This was the Princess of Wales's first official visit to Egypt although she had been briefly to the country once before. On this occasion she was invited by the President's wife so that she could see at first hand some of Mrs Mubarak's social welfare projects in Cairo. In between the official engagements the Princess of Wales was able to visit some of Egypt's many breathtaking sights.

Left: The Princess of Wales at the Temple of Karnak in southern Egypt.

Facing page below left: Meeting 10-year-old Heba Salah at the Institute for Polio and Rehabilitation in Cairo.
Facing page below right and right: The Princess of Wales dressed modestly in a calf-length dress and chiffon silk scarf for her visit to the Al-Azhar Mosque, one of the oldest Islamic universities in the world.

Left: The Princess of Wales admiring ancient Egyptian wall paintings in the tomb of King Seti I in the Valley of the Kings.
Below: Meeting Nagdi Abdo Maboud whose father had worked with Howard Carter, the American archeologist who discovered the tombs of the pharaohs hidden away in the Valley of the Kings.
Facing page above left and right: On the second day of her stay in Cairo the Princess braved the terrific heat to visit one of the seven wonders of the ancient world, the Pyramids at Giza just outside the city. Dressed in pale beige which blended in with the desert sands and the stone Pyramids, she said later, 'It was breathtaking.'
Facing page below: At Karnak Temple, Luxor.
Overleaf: In the Hypostyle Hall at Karnak.

Left: The Duke and Duchess of York with Princess Beatrice and Princess Eugenie at the Royal Windsor Horse Show on 16 May, the first time the family had been seen in public together since the announcement of the Yorks' separation.
Below: The Queen at the wheel of her Land Rover during the Royal Windsor Horse Show.
Facing page: The Princess of Wales was accompanied by the Prince of Wales and their children at the memorial service for her father, the late Earl Spencer, on 19 May.

The Prince and Princess of Wales paid a brief visit to Seville in Southern Spain to attend British National Day at Expo '92 on 21 May.
Above: Touring the British Pavilion after which the Prince and Princess of Wales spent several hours visiting other pavilions on the Expo site.
Left: The Princess of Wales talking to the composer, Sir Andrew Lloyd Webber at a royal gala performance of the British composer's music held at Expo's open-air auditorium.
Facing page: At the Andrew Lloyd Webber royal gala performance.

Left: The Princess Royal riding Desert Orchid, the famous racehorse, for charity at the Windsor International Horse Trials on 24 May.
Right: Zara Phillips at the Horse Trials.
Below: The Princess Royal, who has been President of the Windsor Horse Trials since 1975, presenting prizes at one of the events.

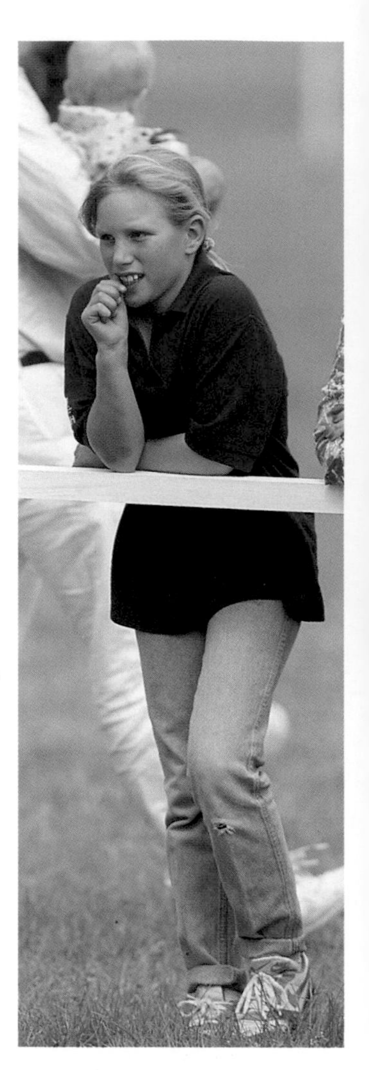

Right: Princess Margaret, President of the NSPCC, attended the charity's Oscar de la Renta fund-raising fashion show at Claridge's Hotel, central London on 1 June.

Below: The Queen Mother opening Ronald Gibson House, a home for elderly people in Tooting, south London on 2 June.

The Derby, first contested in 1780, is the most famous horse race in the world. By tradition it takes place on the first Wednesday in June at Epsom Racecourse south of London. Derby Day is a great day out in the British social calendar and this year the Queen's party included the Duchess of Gloucester (facing page above left) and the Duke of Edinburgh (facing page above right).

Right: the royal party inspecting the horses in the paddock.

The
Ever Ready
Derby

Above left: The Queen wearing a magnificent ruby and diamond tiara in Paris for the first evening of her State Visit to France on 9 June.
Above right: For the second day of the State Visit the Queen wore an elegant blue and white suit by one of her favourite designers, Hardy Amies.
Left: As a mark of respect for his important royal guests President Mitterand offered the Queen and Prince Philip the use of the presidential open-top Citroën, which is only brought out on rare occasions.

Facing page above left: The Queen at the dinner held in honour of President Mitterand at the British Embassy in Paris.
Above right: On the third day of the State Visit the Queen and Prince Philip travelled to the town of Blois in the Loire Valley where they were shown round the magnificent Château by Jack Lang, France's flamboyant Minister for Education and Culture and also mayor of Blois.
Right: From Blois the royal couple flew on to Bordeaux where the Queen and Prince Philip entertained President and Madame Mitterand to dinner on board HMY Britannia.

Facing page above: The Queen at Trooping the Colour on 13 June, the colourful ceremony to mark the sovereign's official birthday which takes place on the second Saturday in June.
Facing page below: After Trooping the Colour the royal family went out on to the balcony of Buckingham Palace to watch the RAF flypast down the Mall and over the Palace.

Right: The Queen Mother, a Lady of the Garter, wearing traditional robes for the Garter Day Service at St George's Chapel, Windsor on 15 June.
Below: The Prince and Princess of Wales return to Windsor Castle by carriage after the Garter Day Service. By tradition the Prince of Wales is one of the twenty-four Knights of the Garter.

The four-day Royal Meeting at Ascot is one of the highlights of both the English racing and social calendars. The packed crowds always cheer the procession of open landaus bringing the Queen and the rest of the royal party from nearby Windsor Castle before the start of each afternoon's racing.
Left: The Queen on her way to view the horses in the paddock.
Below left: The Princess Royal and Princess Margaret driving down the course to the Royal Enclosure on the first day of racing.
Below right: The Princess of Wales at Ascot.
Facing page above: The Queen and Prince Philip on the second day of Royal Ascot.
Facing page below: Princess Margaret wearing striking green and white for the third day of Royal Ascot.

XEROX

CONDICOTE
HILL

Facing page above: The Princess of Wales on a walkabout in Belfast during her visit to Northern Ireland on 29 June.
Facing page below: The Princess Royal, President, Animal Health Trust, taking part in the Animal Fun Day at Ascot racecourse with her children, Peter and Zara Phillips.

On 18 July Lady Helen Windsor, daughter of the Duke and Duchess of Kent, married Mr Tim Taylor, a London art dealer, at St George's Chapel, Windsor.
Left: Lady Helen, in a simple but elegant pearl-white dress embroidered with silver, diamante and pearl, and designed by Catherine Walker, leaves her parents' home, Crocker End House.
Below: Lady Helen and her father, the Duke of Kent, set off for St George's Chapel.

Right: The bride and groom on the steps of St George's Chapel after the marriage ceremony. Below: Members of the bride's and groom's families leaving the Chapel for the reception at Crocker End House. The reception was attended by some 500 guests.